DIET AND NUTRITION
Additives in Food

Deb Turner

Wayland

DIET AND NUTRITION

Additives in Food
Vitamins in Food
Fibre in Food
Sugar in Food

Series editor: Deborah Elliott
Designer: Malcolm Walker
Cover design: Simon Balley
Artwork: John Yates
Cartoons: Maureen Jackson

First published in 1995 by
Wayland (Publishers) Limited
61 Western Road, Hove,
East Sussex, BN3 1JD, England

Text is based on *Additives* in the *Food Facts* Series,
published in 1992

British Library Cataloguing in Publication Data
Turner, Deb
 Additives in food - (Diet and Nutrition Series)
 I. Title   II. Series
 664.06
 ISBN 0 7502 1435 X

Typesetting by Kudos Editorial and Design Services
Printed and bound by Rotolito Lombarda s.p.a. Italy

Contents

Look and taste

Additives are chemicals which are added to food when it is made in factories.

Colours and flavours are often added to make food look and taste better. There are additives which thicken soups and stews and additives which make food last longer.

In the past, people did not have chemical additives. They put salt, vinegar and sugar in their food to stop it going off.

▼ *This drawing shows a factory where meat was put into huge vats of salt. This made the meat safe to eat for many months.*

Processing our food

Processed food has been cooked, dried or canned, or has had some kind of additive added to it. This is done to make the food last longer, or to make it tastier for people to eat.

Nowadays, most people do not buy as much fresh food as people in the past. We shop at large supermarkets, usually once a week. This means that we have to get most of our food in one go. Fresh food has to be eaten straight away, whereas processed food will last for months.

▼ *This strawberry mousse does not have any real strawberries in it. The strawberry taste and the pink colour come from chemicals.*

Tinned and packet foods have labels which tell us where the foods come from and whether or not they have been processed. They also give the sell-by-date, which is the date by which you must eat the food before it goes off.

You could find out more about the food you eat. Next time you go shopping, look at the labels on your favourite foods. You could make a list like the one below.

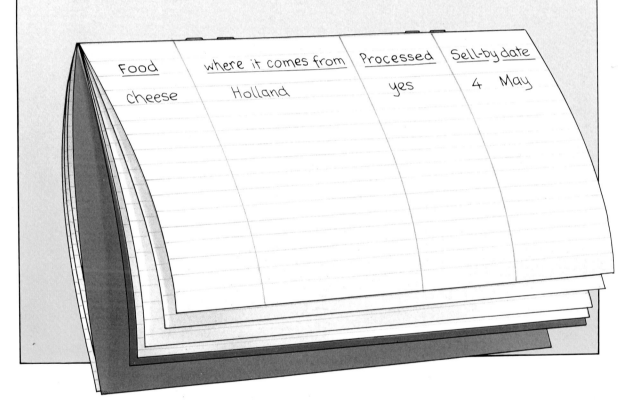

Food	where it comes from	Processed	Sell-by date
Cheese	Holland	yes	4 May

Processing food means it can be made in one country, then sent to another to be sold and eaten. The food will stay fresh.

Processing food can make it look good and taste good. However, it can also make the food much less healthy for us to eat than if the food were fresh.

People who make food to sell are always trying to think up ways to make us like their food so that we will buy more of it. They use more and more additives to make different tastes and colours. They add sugar and fat to food, neither of which are good for us.

Sometimes, too, the way food is processed can take out important vitamins and minerals needed by our bodies.

Cake recipes

Here are two cake recipes. One uses additives and is a chocolate cake. The other cake does not have any additives.

** Always make sure there is an adult around when you are cooking.

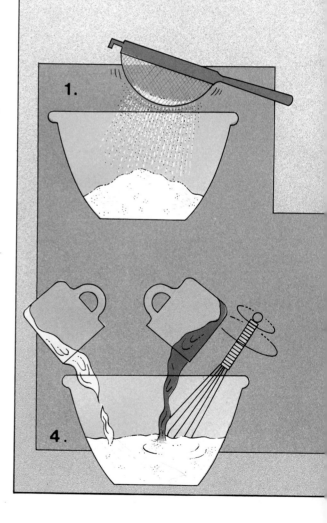

A: Cake with additives
150 g self-raising flour
1/2 teaspoon baking powder
1/2 teaspoon salt
200 g caster sugar
100 g margarine
150 ml milk
2 eggs
1 teaspoon vanilla essence
50 g melted plain chocolate

B: Cake with no additives
150 g plain flour
1/2 teaspoon salt
200 g caster sugar
100 g margarine
150 ml milk
2 eggs

1. For each cake, sift the dry ingredients (flour, sugar and salt, and baking powder for cake A) into a bowl.

2. Add the eggs and margarine, then mix for two minutes. Add the chocolate and vanilla essence to cake A.

3. Pour each mixure into a round cake tin and bake in the oven at 180 ºC/gas mark 4 for about an hour.

You will find that the two cakes look, feel and taste very different.

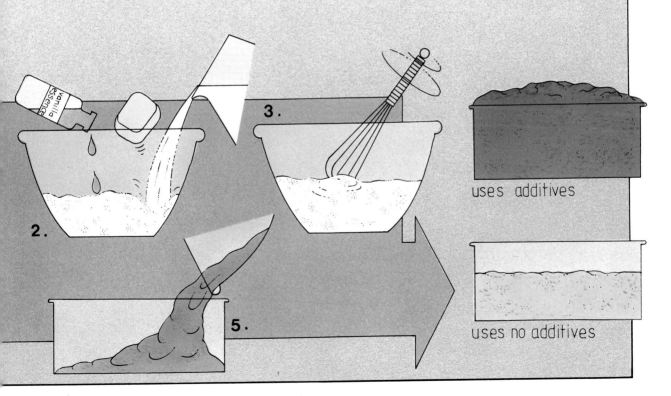

2.

3.

5.

uses additives

uses no additives

Keeping food fresh

▲ *This fruit has been kept for too long. It doesn't look very appetizing, does it?*

Tiny little germs, called bacteria, have spread on the fruit, making it go rotten and mouldy.

There are lots of different kinds of additive. In Britain, twenty-four types are used in food. The additives used to keep food fresh are called preservatives.

Some foods have preservatives in them already. Vinegar, for example, is added to sauces and pickles. It contains an acid which is a preservative.

It is oxygen in the air that makes the bacteria which cause food to go rotten. Additives called antioxidants destroy these bacteria.

▼ *Vitamin C, found in lemon juice, is an antioxidant. For example, slices of apple will go brown after a while. But if you squeeze some lemon juice on to the apple slices, they will not go brown.*

Rotten fruit

You can see how oxygen makes food go rotten. All you need to do is leave out an apple and a banana for a few days.

You will see that each day the pieces of fruit change. The skins wrinkle and change colour. The fruit becomes all soft and squidgy. You could draw the changes you see on a piece of paper.

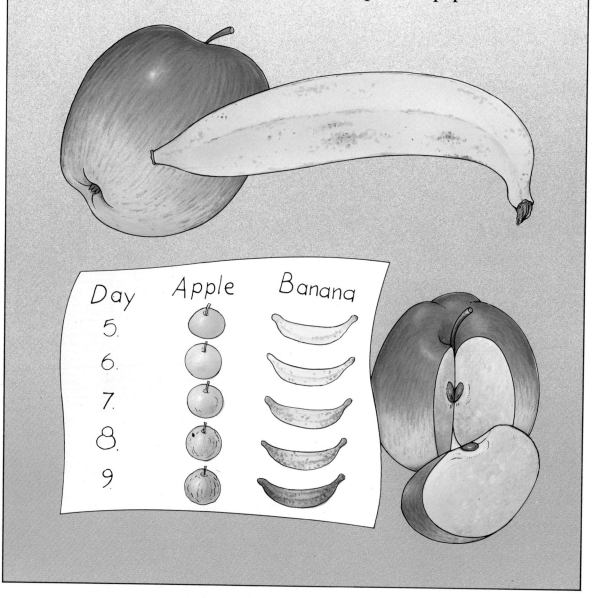

Mixing and thickening

If you add some cooking oil to some water, you will see that they do not mix together. Margarine and mayonnaise have oil and water in them. Special additives called emulsifiers are used to make them mix together.

In the same way as flour is used to thicken sauces, additives called thickeners are put in foods to thicken them. Tinned soups and sauces contain thickeners, for example.

▼ *Both chemical and natural thickeners are used in food. Juice from the bark of acacia trees is used to thicken soups.*

Delicious mayonnaise

We eat mayonnaise in sandwiches and with salads and burgers.
This recipe for mayonnaise uses an egg yolk to make the different
ingredients stick together.

You will need:
1 egg yolk
1 teaspoon French mustard
150 ml olive oil
white vinegar
a pinch of salt and pepper

1. Mix together the egg yolk, mustard, salt and pepper.
2. While stirring the mixture, add the olive oil a drop at a time.
Try not to pour in too much oil in one go, otherwise the
mayonnaise will not thicken.
3. Stir in the white vinegar until the mayonnaise becomes smooth.

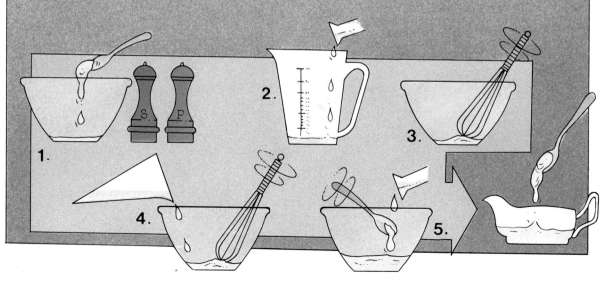

Colourings

▶ *Crushed cochineal beetles give a red dye which is used to colour food.*

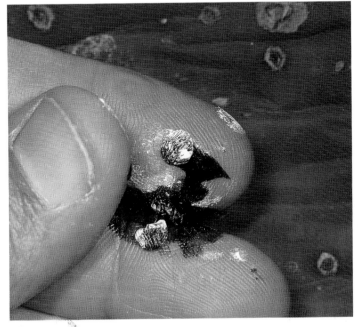

Many foods do not look very appetizing unless they have had colours added. Biscuits, sweets and ice-cream might look very pale and boring without colouring.

Colourings can be natural, like the red from beetroot and the orange from carrots. But most of the colourings used in processed foods are chemicals.

▲ *The fruit jellies in this photograph have been made in the shape of real fruit. They have had chemicals added to them too, which have given them fruit colourings.*

Although chemical colourings do make food look more interesting, some can be harmful. Children who drink too much orange squash, for example, can become hyperactive. They find it hard to keep still and to sleep at night. This is because the squash has had a yellow colouring added.

16

Some people who eat too many foods with additives suffer from headaches and rashes.

The jellies in the photograph opposite were coloured to look like real fruit. This is because sweet-makers believe that if a sweet has a fruit flavouring, it should have the fruit colouring, too. What do you think? Try the experiment below to find out.

Making sweets

Whisk together 300 g of icing sugar and the white of one egg. You will need some orange and yellow food colouring and lemon and orange flavouring, which you can buy from a supermarket.

Divide your sweet mixture into two. Add a few drops of the yellow colouring and the orange flavouring to one half. Add the lemon flavouring and the orange colouring to the other half. Mix up each mixture. Then roll the mixture into small, bite-sized pieces.

Give one yellow and one orange sweet to a friend and ask him or her to guess the flavours. If your friend gets it wrong, it is because they imagine the yellow sweet will taste of lemon and the orange sweet will taste of orange.

► These are battery hens. They are kept in small cages and are not free to walk about and find their own food.

Next time you eat an egg, check if it is from a battery hen. If so, then the golden-yellow colour is not real. It is an additive.

Battery hens' eggs do not have rich, golden yolks. The hens are fed a certain type of grain which does not have any natural colour, so the yolks are very pale. Farmers add red or yellow colouring to the grain to change the colour of the yolk to golden yellow.

Different flavours

When something is said to have a certain flavour, such as a rhubarb and custard sweet, or a sherbet lemon, it might not have any rhubarb, custard or lemon in it. The flavouring may be chemicals made up of lots of other ingredients.

Banana milkshake

Do you like milkshake? If so, you will love this recipe, which uses real fruit flavouring.

You will need:

1/2 litre milk
2 large bananas

Mash up the bananas using a fork. Add the milk, then whisk the mixture until it is smooth and frothy. Pour the milkshake into two tall glasses. Delicious!

There are over 3,000 different flavourings. Only a very small amount of flavouring is used in food. In fact, the amount of flavouring used is usually about 1,000 times smaller than the amount of preservative.

Flavourings are safe to eat, unlike some colourings and preservatives which can make people ill.

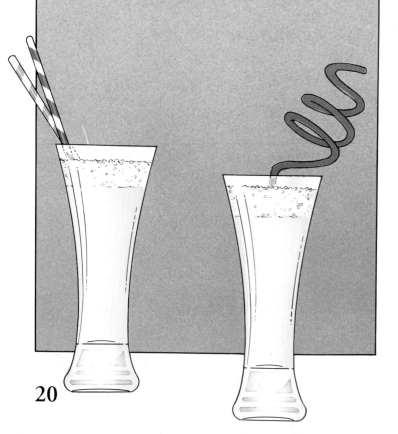

▲ *The flavour enhancer MSG is made from wheat or sugar beet.*

There are also additives which add to the flavours in food, making it taste stronger. These are called flavour enhancers. Monosodium glutamate, or MSG, is a flavour enhancer which is used a lot in Chinese cooking.

Allergies

◄ *People who are allergic to shellfish, nuts and strawberries might be violently sick or get a very red rash on their skin if they eat these foods.*

If you have a food allergy, it means that you become ill or get a rash on your skin if you eat a certain food. Cows' milk, eggs, wheat and citrus fruits are foods that many people are allergic to.

Some people are allergic to chemical additives. On page 16, we read how children can be affected by food colourings. It is also true that children who eat too many foods with additives find that they cannot sleep properly and get angry very easily.

▼ *The best and most healthy diet is one which has natural foods without additives. This meal of meat, vegetables, rice and fruit is fresh and tastes delicious without the help of flavourings or colourings.*

We have seen that additives are added to processed food. However, sometimes fresh food has come into contact with a type of additive. Almost all fruit and vegetables are sprayed with chemicals called pesticides when they are growing. These kill any insects living on the foods.

There is a slight chance that someone could become ill if he or she eats food sprayed with pesticide. That is why it is important to wash all fruit and vegetables carefully.

► *This farmer is spraying pesticide on to his growing fruit.*

E numbers

Next time you go to a supermarket, look at the lists of
ingredients on some tins and packets of food. The full
chemical name of the additives used may be put down or they
may be listed as numbers with an 'E' in front.

The E numbers may include preservatives, colours, emulsifiers
and stabilizers.

▲ *When you are buying a food which is 'fruit flavoured', for example, look at the list of ingredients to make sure real fruit, and not flavourings, has been added.*

Many countries have rules about which additives can be used in food. This stops food-makers using additives which might be harmful.

Food-makers use different recipes and add different flavourings and colourings to their products. You can see this for yourself by looking at different makes of a type of soup. Remember that some additives are listed as chemicals and some as E numbers.

This exercise should help you to work out which makes of food are the healthiest.

Ingredients: water, potato, carrot, mutton, onion, beef, pearl barley, salt, soya protein (1%) natural gum (guar xanthan), mutton bouillon, sugar, herbs, citric acid.

Ingredients: water, potatoes, carrots, onions, beef, peas, modified cornflour, tomato pure'e, salt, yeast extract, sodium glutamate, spices, herbs colour-caramel.

Choosing food

▼ *Eating should be enjoyable, but shopping should be quite a serious business. Make sure that you and your family know what is in the food you are eating.*

The best kind of diet is one which is balanced. This means that you eat lots of different types of food. It is all right to eat sweets and chocolate sometimes, as long as you eat plenty of fresh fruit and vegetables.

Most additives will not cause you any harm, but it is better to have as few additives as possible in your diet. Eating plenty of fresh food keeps you fit and healthy.

Glossary

allergy   If you sneeze when you are in a dusty room or you become ill when you eat a certain food, you are said to have an allergy.

appetizing   Looks or smells good to eat.

chemicals   Substances which are mixed together to make a different substance.

fat   White or yellow greasy substance.

processed food   Food which has had things added to it.

sell-by-date   The date you must eat food by, otherwise it will go off.

vats   Very large containers for putting liquids or foods in.

Books to read

A Picnic of Poetry selected by Anne Harvey (Blackie, 1988/ Puffin, 1990)

A-Z: Food by Beverley Mathias and Ruth Thomson (Franklin Watts, 1991)

Food by Kay Davies and Wendy Oldfield (Wayland, 1990)

Food and Diet (Heinemann Children's Reference, 1990)

Food Hygiene by Pete Sanders (Franklin Watts, 1990)

Keep Out of the Kitchen, Mum by Jill Cox (Deutsch, 1991)

Poems About Food selected by A. Earl and D. Sensier (Wayland, 1994)

What's Cooking? by Gabrielle Woolfitt (Wayland, 1994)

Picture acknowledgements
APM cover; Ardea 15; Bruce Coleman 13; Chapel Studios 6, 11, 19, 22, 23; Jeff Greenberg 25, 28; Hulton 4-5; Hutchison 18, 21, 24; Wayland Picture Library 10, 16; Zefa 26.
The cover photograph was styled by Zoe Hargreaves.

Index